# Voice Memos, Sticky Notes, and Unsent Texts

## Caitlin Allen

BookLeaf
Publishing

India | USA | UK

Presentation by *BookLeaf Publishing*

Web: www.bookleafpub.com

E-mail: info@bookleafpub.com

ISBN : 9789357448208

First edition 2021

# DEDICATION

If you know me, and you're reading this, please talk about literally anything else with me the next time you see me. And every time after that.

If you don't know me, well, I hope it makes you feel a little less alone.

# ACKNOWLEDGEMENT

Shout-out to my partner and my D&D group for telling me I should do this despite knowing I haven't finished a single project in over 18 months. Your faith in me is unnerving but appreciated.

# PREFACE

I talk about mental health issues a lot. These are almost all sad thoughts I had while laying alone in the dark. Most of which have never been shared before. Proceed with caution I guess. And thanks for trying.

# unsure

Sometimes I think it would be easier to turn
around and run back into the darkness.
something about the light,
while it's beautiful,
I just never feel at home in it.
I think it's because I've spent so long in the dark
that I'm still a little scared of the sun.
I know that I should go forward,
toward the light,
toward something new and different,
something better and something safer,
but something about the darkness calls me
and swallows me like a riptide
and brings me back into the darkness.
it's crazy to think that on a black ocean under a
starless sky is a place where I could feel safe,
or at least where things are familiar.
it's on days like this where I'm existing in the
twilight that I don't know if I'm getting better or
getting worse,
if I'm lying to myself or if I'm lying to everyone
else.
I don't know what I'm supposed to do here.
I know what I should do. I don't know what I
will do.

all I know
is that some part of me isn't ready to
leave the darkness
and some part of me is still afraid of the light.

# choose

Sometimes in life, there's not a best choice or a
right answer. Sometimes you just have to live
and see what the lesson is in retrospect. Life is a
path with no one destination, and though we
may try to use maps and follow signs, we'll
never end up quite where we thought we would -
but we'll end up with memories and a story to
tell. You get to choose how this chapter of your
life goes. No right or wrong. It's not black or
white. You can go and leave early if you're not
having fun. You can stay and change your mind
and go on your own. You can sit here in
indecision. No one can make this choice but
you, and that's the beauty and the horror of
living. But rejoice in the fact that there is no
right or wrong answer. Just choose the next step.
Tomorrow will come, and you'll meet it when it
does. Just take your next step.

# To the man who loved me first,

To the man who loved me first,

I'm not 16 anymore. I'm not the person you once loved and I'm not the person who once loved you. 5 years have passed but I feel as though I have aged a lifetime.

You knew me once. I'd like for you to know me again, and for our lives to entangle again in a new way. We were strangers, we were friends, we were lovers, we were strangers. It's time to be friends again.

So, to the man who loved me first, here's a few things I thought you should know:

1. I write now. Apparently, I'm fairly good at it. I finally wrote those short stories that I thought I could never finish.
2. You were right, Rick and Morty is a good show.

3. In one of my labs, I made cancer. Believe it or not, it's way lamer than it sounds.

4. I missed you. I missed my friend.

5. I still do puzzles. The difference is now I finish them.

6. I still have our memory boxes. I couldn't bring myself to throw them away.

7. I looked at them not too long ago. I think you might want your prom handkerchief back.

8. I repainted my room, then moved in Mike's old room anyways.

9. Mike is engaged now.

10. Chris moved to Texas.

11. Junior had another baby.

12. I've kissed more girls than boys now.

13. Remember how awkward I was about sex? I'm now the wikipedia of sex ed for my friends

14. I still play DnD.

15. I think of your parents a lot.

16. I wonder if they ever forgave me.

17. I'm glad you did.

18. It took me a year after we broke up to eat at a Wendy's again.

19. My favorite color is blue.

20. I got really into baseball caps???

21. My socks match now - I'm mature

22. I got scammed by a sugar momma

23. I still paint. And I think I still have the paintings we started together but never finished.

24. I was so mad at you for wasting those canvases.

25. I finally learned how to be okay with people not liking me.

26. A week after we broke up, a French guy invited me to a movie festival in Florida with him. I didn't go but I can't believe I considered it for so long

27. 4 days after we broke up, Emma told me I'm bi. Turns out it's *not* a normal, straight thing to just think women are amazing and that you want to kiss them all the time. Who knew?

28. I want to get a couple tattoos.

29. I think about Jasper a weird amount. Like why did he sit like that on the couch??? Incredible

30. I'm not afraid of heights anymore

31. I'm sorry I snipped at you during our AP English presentation on Crime and Punishment

32. I figured out Mr. German's middle name is Patsy!

33. every time I heard there was an accident in our area, I checked to make sure it wasn't you.

34. Words can't express how sorry I am that this one was.

35. I've seen god and I'm not afraid anymore.

36. I dislocated my shoulder and sometimes it just falls out of the socket.

37. I threw a couple out of Cracker Barrel for being blatantly homophobic and it is possibly the single proudest thing I've done in my career so far.

38. I know way too much about animal genitalia now. Specifically, duck penises.

39. I think this list will either be really well received or I will regret writing this for all of eternity because of the cringe factor, but fuck it, it's 1am and I got inspired.

40. Every time I put on a bathing suit I think of that creep at Ohiopyle.

41. I get sad sometimes and I don't know why.

42. I know why, but I can't control it.

43. I used your hulu account for like 6 months after we broke up and I do not regret it

44. I love Jack so much that my heart can't contain it.

45. I sincerely want you to be happy

46. I came home one weekend and saw you mowing a random lawn on 136 and almost wrecked because it was the first time I had seen you in 2 years.

47. The Celtic knot necklace is still my favorite. I wear it often

48. I need like 6 alarms to wake up in the morning

49. I tried to buy stocks and IMMEDIATELY lost money

50. I can't help but smile when I watch La La
Land
51. I dance. Not professionally, I'm still an idiot,
I just don't care anymore.
52. I hope we can catch up sometime, in person.
I want to hear about the man you became.


To the man who loved me first,
From the girl who broke your heart

# stardust

I'm made of stardust -
We all are.
We have the inner spark of a thousand galaxies
burning bright within us. The very atoms that
make us up have traveled billions of miles to
combine into the unique masterpiece that we are.
We are made of a million little coincidences and
mishaps. We were born from collapsing
supernovas. I'm the very embodiment of a
trillion suns.
Maybe that's why I feel like exploding.

# burning

I'll say that I don't care, I'll let the world burn
But the truth is that I burn for the world
I burn in my solitude
In my sadness
I burn in my grief
And in my dismay
I burn for the people I love
And for the ones I'll never meet
The truth is
I'd burn myself alive every single day for the
world
But no one would burn for me

# empty again

There's something about being a giver
that leaves you with nothing
somehow
no matter how you try to ration things
or rationalize them
even if you only give the smallest bits
you always end up empty-handed
because when you're a giver
you don't know how to do anything but pour
into others
and you never see the risk in giving
until you yourself
are empty

# i am a mushroom

There's light, filtering through the dancing
leaves
Swirling, falling, a lilting song no one can hear
I sit, here, in the wet, in the dark, in the damp
and in the muddy,
Staring at the heavens of green and their golden
dresses,
Never privy to that touch,
And it is heaven here.
I watch the grass grow each and every moment
from this corner of my world
I see the seeds fall in the Fall, I watch with
curious eyes which will grow into the cold air
and which is sent to the warmth of the dirt. To
return promptly to it's ancient home
The world walks by, unaware of the universe
under their feet, staring above and dreaming of
the stars,
When the secrets of the universe are the essence
of this planet.
When I am just as important, just as worthy, as
the birth of a new star.
I am what returns the dead to the building blocks
of light, i am the mother of rebirth, i am at home
in the dark and i carry the burden of the  cold

and the damp and the dirty,. As you stay dry, and
I relish in my place. I see birth and death not as
opposites but as pieces of a circle, standing hand
in hand. I am the hooded figure of nature, I stand
with face covered as if i were Death himself. But
I am more than death. I am the bridge and the
heart of life.
I stand in the blackness, the inky pool of
nothingness, the eternal night. And i scream in
my brightest colors, in my most magnificent
shapes and forms and I stand as I please.
I revolt against being nothing but know that i too
will cease and another will return me to cycle. I
know what it means to live because i have stood
in the shoes of death, played every part in the
universal play.

# what i want

I want to make you feel alive again. I want you to feel the sunshine on your skin and know in your core that it has traveled millions of miles just to kiss your skin. No one else's. I want your hair to whip around you and make you feel like you're flying and falling all at once. I want you to stare at the stars and feel their gravity pulling you in. I want cold water pulsing through your veins, I want gasps of airy laughter, I want the fire to lick your lips and make you say "Let's do it again". I want you to be so in love with the feeling of being alive that you crave it in the mundane. I want you to take a sip of tea and feel like you're reborn. I want you to smile at the bird outside your window. I want you to feel the grass between your toes and crave the body of the earth against yours. I want you to find what lights your soul and makes you so utterly in love with living that it will carry you through the hard days, the tough weeks, the miserable months. I want you to find something that makes your soul vibrate and makes you look forward to the possibilities. Because that's how I did it. That's why I'm still here. I know things will get bad again. Maybe things are bad right now. But as long as I find something to love, something small, ordinary, mundane - as long as I have that, I have a reason to live.

# 3:21 AM

even my sleep paralysis demon forgot about me.

# self harm

I hurt myself with invisible razors. My wrists, I knew, would be too obvious. But cutting myself down, killing myself from the inside out, tearing my own heart from my chest? That's something you can hide. And with every piece of yourself that you cut away, the mask would be easier to put on. By the time people notice, you'll have been a shell longer than you know. You'll be too good at hiding to find yourself again.

# my heart is yours

please
rip my heart out
take it

please
if you love me,
take away this pain. if you loved me, you'd stop
my suffering
please
let me go. this heart is pain.
let me have peace.

if you ever loved me, or ever could,
please
rip my heart out

# roleplaying is therapy

"You can't change the way the wind blows, but you can always adjust your sails to find a new direction."

how is my DND character better at coping than I am?

# in the eye's mind

when my dogs get spooked at night, I worry my
monsters are real, and they can see them too.

# love to give

I think I have too much love to give.
Even when I am angry or overwhelmed, it's
because there's something I want to do or
someone I want to help, a way I want to share
my love. Maybe that's why I read and write and
paint -- if I can pour my extra love into these
passions, my heart can't be broken as easily. But
I know it's a bandaid on a broken bone. No
matter what I do, I always come back to finding
people to pour my love into. I fall so helplessly
in love with strangers, I lust after baristas in
roadside cafes, I pour my heart into every
crevice I come across so naturally. It's like I was
built to share love, but never spare any of it for
myself. And try as I might, I know I'll break my
own heart day after day, by giving my love to
people who don't deserve it. I have so much love
to give, and still, I'm not sure if anyone actually
wants it.

# monday afternoon

I feel it again. That awful feeling in my veins, the feeling of a thousand whispers telling me I'm not good enough, the echoes of every evil that I've experienced, the push to feel

Pain.

I want to hurt myself. I clench my fist, digging my nails into my skin, trying not to cry. I don't want to hurt myself. I know it would be bad. It's not healthy. It's dangerous. I'm better than that aren't I?

I'm not so sure anymore.

I feel my pace quicken as my brain reminds me where I keep my knives, where the closest stairwell I could throw myself down is, where the parking garage I had planned to jump off is -

And I unclench my fist. I don't want that anymore. I like life. I'm feeling horrible right now. Like I don't deserve the air I breathe or the food I eat. But I try to shout over the whispers dancing beneath my skin that I'm worth

something. Someone cares about me. Someday
I'll be happy again.

I think about the sunshine. The feel of golden
light on my skin as I sprawl in the grass. I think
about my parents. Movie nights snuggling
between them. I remind myself why life is good.

I still want to feel pain, but maybe what I need
most is to feel loved without guilt.

# fungi

Oh how I envy the mushrooms
how I envy such a creature
such a being of endless possibilities
of 1 million different forms all beautiful in their
own rights
I envy that they can grow anywhere
how I envy their powers to take living things and
break them down and build something new
how I envy the regeneration
how I envy their ability to see beauty and death
and grow in the darkness
oh how I envy the mushrooms
the fungi
the things that people never look at
how I wish to be envied just like those little
mushrooms
how I wish I could be looked at the same way
I can't take the broken and dying things to make
them beautiful again
all I can do is pretend that I can come in 1
million different forms when I just always will
be who I am
somehow looking at mushrooms I see something
that I wish I could be

I see the possibilities of everything I'm not

mushrooms prove beautiful things can grow in
the dark
but I am not one of them

# i just have to try

As much as I wish there was an easy way out, a hero to save me from the impending darkness, I know there isn't. I need to save myself. And I will, but not before I fail a thousand times more.

# remember

Remember how that used to feel? That rollercoaster of emotion we had? The times where our lips would almost touch, our arms held each other close, our eyes held each other and sparkled brighter than any star in the sky. Do you remember how we loved one another, dreamt of a future full of adventures together? We had such plans, made beautiful promises.

Do you remember how our love died?

Do you remember the anger, and the pain, and the tears? Do you remember how dark our lives got, how we blamed each other for the slow drip of our veins? We swam together and we sank together -- that was our life together. No calm seas, just waves that carried us high before shattering us against the rocks. Do you remember the sheer power of the emotions we felt? Sometimes I crave that high again, but I know it will always end with my shattered heart.

But still, I remember.

# girls

Some girls are dangerous like a knife, cold,
sharp, words cutting into your soul and leaving
you drained.

Some girls are dangerous like a storm, rolling in
slow, then tearing it all apart right before your
eyes.

Some girls are dangerous like lions, like war,
like a wreck -- but me?

I'm dangerous like a heart attack.
I give you life. I give you love and warmth and a
beat to dance through life to. And one day, I'll
decide to end the dance and leave you lying on
the floor gasping for air.

# keep going

Just because I've accepted where I'm at doesn't
mean I've forgotten where I'm going. I'm
resting, not stopping.

# word vomit

poetry is so stupid sometimes.
i can write and write and write and spill all the
thoughts in my head, filling pages with
desperate squiggles, begging to be understood
and to be loved. i can write for hours on end and
unravel the complexities of my mind, and at the
end of it all, I'm just sitting there empty, thinking
that maybe, just maybe, someone will read it and
know who i am. but it's really just stupid. stupid
to hope that anyone could ever feel how i feel
and know the depths of my emotions. stupid to
think that even if my words weren't hidden away
in the dark, someone would dust them off and
use them as a map to my soul. stupid to think
that i could ever be loved when all i am is a just
another human writing shitty poetry in the dark.